SWEET BREATH

of

KNOWING

Theresa May Evie

Outskirts Press, Inc.
Denver, Colorado

Sweet Breath of Knowing
All Rights Reserved.
Copyright © 2007 Theresa May Evie
V3.0

Illustrations by Sandra K. Nikirk

Cover Photo © 2009 JupiterImages Corporation. All rights reserved - used with permission.

Outskirts Press, Inc.
http://www.outskirtspress.com

Paperback ISBN: 978-1-4327-3205-9
Hardback ISBN: 978-1-4327-3395-7

Library of Congress Control Number: 2009920236

Outskirts Press and the "OP" logo are trademarks belonging to Outskirts Press, Inc.

PRINTED IN THE UNITED STATES OF AMERICA

DEDICATED TO THE MEMORY OF

the women of the past
centuries that have held
humanity together through
an unrelenting assault on
the spirit of innocence that
we call upon today to save us.

author

"All that we see or seem,
is but a dream within a dream."
E. A. Poe

If you are a young human
being, you already know
this makes perfect sense.
In fact, the younger
you may be, the more these
words touch a place in
your mind that confirm,
the opening moments of
life began a dilemma
of reality that becomes
more complex than
you expected while
in the spirit…

Nothing is what it
appears to be… Nothing.

At birth our life spirit
is suddenly ours to protect
while we are barely aware
we exist...
If you are an infant
human being, you are the
envy of everyone
you touch... The sweet
breath that carries your
soul outward is deeply
inhaled and cherished
by all you become close to...

The very atoms of your
being, now being exchanged
with the outer world,
are the newest soul
of all infants before
you since the beginning
of humankind… Each
exchange of the most
basic stuff of life being
created in your little body
is released to find its
spirit with the stars,
the spirit of all that is
alive today and the
very breath of god itself…

Nothing seems like it
really is… Nothing.

The very essence of the
air is the very essence
of the stars transformed
only by the breath of life…
All the lives that lived have
contributed to the very
being of each life today...

If you are a young
human being, you
already know this.

That knowing is the most
precious thing you will ever
have in life! The real
human goal is to keep it
alive and allow it to flourish
in the love of other lives
that share your spirit…
This will be the most
difficult challenge of living
a human life… Everything
that seems to be human
is in reality a pulling away
of the very breath we need
to cherish…

If you are a young
human being, you
already know…

The dust from the furthest
star, far flung elements
from the long broken comets,
the last granules from
the oldest eroded mountain,
and the smallest life-forms
from the deepest sea
are combined with the very
breath of the child
to continue the cycle
of life's spirit that
creates itself and depends
upon its creating to create
again…

If you are a young
human being, you
already know this.

Time is the measure of
how the life spirit
is drawing on itself
to bring the complete
force of love back
together from the
moments of human
collective life that have
allowed the love spirit
to continually diminish
from the very instant
human life erupted…
But now the time is, that
the cycle begins anew…

Yes, now is the time
that the cycle begins
anew… the strength
of the spirit of human
touch and love is
again pulling us back
from the edge…

If you are a young
human being, you
already know…

So if the youngest of life's
caring creatures is charged
with the re-creating and
retracting of the life and
love spirit among all
that is and will be, we
must step aside and
allow this spirit to flourish
and connect with all
of the same, and this will
become the newest form
of human life itself!!

Nothing is what
it seems to be…

If you could see the person
writing these words, you
would find a grey old soul...
But there is a caption
that reads: "We are always
the same age inside," and
because of this truth it
has remained possible for
someone with a weary
life of trials and mistakes
to feel that young
human being "knowing"
that life is of life itself...
And this old life is
connected in the same

young human spirit that
will combine with yours
to recreate the love spirit
condition that must come…

What is available from
those of us is the
truth about what is
real and what is
human life's fallacies.
And because it is these
fallacies themselves that
have diminished the
very life spirit, it is
time for us to dispel

the illusions that form
the life around your
young human spirit, and
hence, you may recognize
the illusion for what
it is and use its weight
against it to begin our
change of spirit growth,
and stop the evolution
of spirit death… If you
are a young human
being, we that carry
the remnants of
the love spirit of life
welcome you.

Each time you encounter
some of life's illusions
herein revealed, you
will have the knowledge
of those past to make
of the deceptions
what really is… These
thoughts that manifest
from a difficult testing
of the life spirit will in
some measure help
shatter the spirit of
greed, hate and despair
that have flung the
elements of life back
into the shadow spirit cycle
since the beginning of
mankind…

If you are a young
human being the
breath you breathe
today will be the
beginning of a new
human evolution.

There seem to be only a
handful of phases in
life that must be
understood for what
they actually are to
push open the shroud
of deception that has
made the human life
one that must be
endured to be enjoyed…

The dignity of God spirit
within has become
veiled in a shadow
of mistrust and deception
that has stalled the
love spirit from recreating,
and left unchecked,
will be our ultimate failure
if the light of dignity
cannot be spread again
by these young messengers
of love and life.

If you are a young human
being, listen to these
lessons from the shadows,
so that you may not spend
precious moments of
life struggling against
the illusions, but instead
look past it all with
the love and life spirit
intact…

Family

The moment you emerged
from the spirit realm
into this light; In
China, Brazil, Africa,
Indonesia and throughout
the globe, others'
dusk, twilight, dawn,
and midnight birth
join your entry into
this human form… They
too came with only the
knowing of the spirit and
were also thrust into the
arms and lives of people
unknown before (because
parents and children do
not share previous spirits,

the communion of all love
must emerge from spirit
to spirit without clouds
of known union) this is
how the re-creation of the
human mind will transform
mankind… when all spirits
fuel each other, without
conceived notions, but
simply the innocence of
newborn crib-mates.
Therefore, into this light
you emerged and are
presented as a human
being in whole... Your
family is introduced to you
and you to them…

This is a profound
spiritual moment…
You are still bound to the
creator spirit and now
suddenly achieve the
human spirit connection
with the woman that
has nurtured and given
you form from her
form… This begins the
human process of shared
intimacy that is known
only between you and her…
There is no experience ahead
that will duplicate this…
But you are now open

to the shared intimacy
between humans that
your God spirit created
you to inspire, nurture,
and give away… But
now it also begins that
everything is not as it
seems… this very person
that gave you birth and
is charged with providing
a place in life for your
spirit to flourish, may
herself only have a fleeting
memory of the very God
spirit that glows from
your child body, that
profound love light of life.

She and the father of
the child, as well as all
those connected in the
family bond of existence
(except those who are
still children), may have
lost much of the very
spirit that you are…
However, they and all
the adults in contact with
this infant child are drawn
in the most profound,
deep, and longing measure
to connect with your
living union with the
creator God spirit. Some
are fully aware of your
creator connection and
bond immediately with
the spirit of union.

Some have regrettably lost
the knowledge that
the very communion
that draws them to you
is still alive and available
in each of them. If only
they had the means to
negate all that humankind
has burdened them
with over the hardened
years of life. We must
remember that the negative
influences of human life
can be so devastating for
some participants that
even the gift of this

powerful God-spirit child
that cannot dispel the negative
emotions, intimately woven
in their body, so much so
that fear and distrust
for life itself may drive
them away from the
child. However, the
love spirit bestowed
by the creator God remains
in your child spirit
always, and now more
than ever, since the
dawn of humanity, the

communion with those
children of your dawn
is open in the magic
fields of space and
quantum waves that
before this time kept
the children's love spirit
confined and constricted
from expanding... The
world, in all its failings,
is being guided to create
the cyber realm that
makes it possible for you
to be with each other...

There is unfathomable
depth to the dynamics
of the human bond…
You have within you the
insight for selective
communion and for
salvation of the love
spirit; that must remain
intact… All the people
in your near and extended
family are driven by many
spirits from their past…
Every waking moment
each is pulled in many
emotional ways that
separate them from the

very spirit you feel in your
soul… The love spirit
is still in each of them
but for some adults,
it has been stretched
fiber thin, and the
continuous drain of life's
struggles prevents it
from retracting once
again to the love and
acceptance that lives
so easily in your
soul. You will recognize
in the oldest of your
family the sense of
renewed spirit connection

because the trials of life
have mostly passed
and only the mission
of departure looms.
Some of these older
ones are allowing
the love spirit
to re-create itself in their
beings, so they can
again absorb the
communion of life and
pass it on.

It is often the most
tragic of all human
failures that children
of the love spirit are
thrust upon the parents
at the very stage of life
when the parents are
required to give completely
of all they are to sustain the
new child, while they
themselves are in the most
active human bondage of
being pulled apart by everything

necessary to sustain the human form. While they struggle to keep their own spirit intact, the needs compounded by the new lives they are now responsible for can drain the very essence they need to remain whole and stretch the veil into the thinnest of net that must sustain both spirit and human wants for everyone including themselves. Therefore,

the parents are, by today's
human design, often
struggling to keep
the veil of dignity and
pure love of self and
life intact and flourishing…
Struggling not out of
lack of passion for the
desire, but out of human
bondage of life's requirements.
Emotions, body, and spirit
can be taken over by the
sheer demands of
existence… But the
love spirit remains

and constantly surfaces
to connect again and
realign with the child
and other like adults. It
is kept somehow intact
by the sheer strength of
the longing to be in
touch with the creator
spirit that you the
child, have naturally
in your awakened soul…
So no matter how removed
from your life the parents
seem to be pulled, love is
a life force that keeps
the connection alive and

will often become
most treasured and
apparent in the
tragic and difficult
moments the child is
given to endure…
The siblings and children
of the extended family
can become your
sustainable connection
to the love spirit because
they are closest to the
very breath of life but
still removed from the
necessities of being an

adult human form…
However, as they
get further along in life they
too are beginning to be
stretched in spirit to
contain the failings they
have encountered in
their perception of their
senses and have had
to alter their spirit of
emotion and trust to
keep intact their own
veil of spirit, so they can
survive the human material
attack that is soon to come…

These siblings, cousins, and parents, along with the older members and the adults of the child spirit, will reveal themselves to you and offer the communion bond that will remain a branch you can hold to when the assault of the negative spirit of life is thrown upon you… Keep close the positive loving people given to you…they are your insight into the beauty of humanity and the living connection to the creative energy and passion of the creator God itself.

School

Here is the beginning
of the proof that life is
really not what it seems
to be… In this greatest
element of human progress
you are presented with
the unfolding of all that
we know about ourselves
and the energy we live
within… Now you will
learn the very forms
of wave and particle
energy that combine to
present themselves to
us in every part of life…

The elements from the
distant past that lost their
light so we could gain
our own. Also, you will find
the intellectual forms that
evolved in our spirit.
Those that work against
and with progressive
elements of the courses
of light and shadow
alike… everything
that is written already
is alive in your light
spirit, all these elemental

quantum activities are
alive in the spirit…
the very ability of
humankind to construct
the theories and project
their realities brings us
closer to the realm of
the spirit of light…
Within this part of life
we know as school we
can find the most
beautiful touch of the
human heart… Here we
offer to the love spirit

of the child, all we have
been able to glean from
the human experience…
Through beauty and tragedy,
anger and compassion,
the fear of each other
and the sheer joy of
human intimacy… all
that is, is open for
your review… and as
the spirit of love would
have it, the teachers
that brings this to you
in the early and childhood
years are without dispute,

the persons that remain
alive in the child spirit,
and are open to your
communion and heart
in response… Somewhere in
the early years of
knowledge, often at a
younger age that many
teachers expect, you will
have a "knowing" of
your life's direction; this
will come to you in the
spirit of knowing that
cannot be questioned or
explained; it will be

the revelation of the
life gift that you
will eventually explore
and develop… Please
take this knowing and
place it in your heart
and mind as soon as
it presents itself… This
is your life's love and
with the first chance to
inform your closest
people in life it should
be expressed, do not be
dissuaded, even if
discouraged, keep it hard
in a place in your being

that can be opened when
you are free to make
your own decisions… You
see the knowledge and
experience of human
development presented
in the education process
is your window to your
human spirit… When
you "know," you will
know. Then you will
be at the point again
where your love spirit will
be defined and if you
must, or decide to, depart
from this path it will

begin to stretch the veil
of love and prepare the
way for the shroud of
shadow to weaken your
spirit of light… It may
take a lifetime to find
your way back to this
"heart" place of knowing…
You see the spirit is the
real meaning of life and
if your spirit calling
is of one nature and you
go, or are forced to go,
elsewhere, you must always
keep the real nature of

your spirit alive so you
can find your way back,
and not allow the shadow
to diminish or darken the
path to your true light…
There are teachers that
know this and will help you
to get there, there are
others that no longer
have this light within,
they will easily reveal
themselves to you and
may only be there to
present the learning

and subject matter, but their shadow should be avoided always... The other very critical heart element of the school experience is the interaction between spirits of your own (or near) age... This is the hardest part of human development, in every step toward the age of reason, adolescence and young adulthood you will be driven away from each other in ways that probably will be

recalled throughout your life… The dynamics of maturing from stage to stage, with all the family, people, spirit, and human emotions drawing you to various ways of seeing and believing, are drawing every one of your friends and peers from within themselves in the same variety of ways. This creates a high energy field that is pulsating, both magnetic and expanding and will

find rest in many places
and configurations…
Those spirits of your
early childhood may often
find a place in your total
life, the further you
age from the child spirit
the weaker the spirit
bond, until in early
adult life the attraction /
repulsion cycle will repeat,
often daily, before the
spirit rhythms coincide
and you find the friends
and loved ones that
will share your energy,

because they are tuned to
your very spirit cycle…
Much of this happens in
the school environment
of the young human beings.
It will continue in a lesser
way, into the higher learning
years, but the forced human
exchange that this stage
of life provides is a very
profound means of spirit
exchange, acceptance, and
rejection that furthers the love
spirit's gentle envelopment
of the human evolution…

Society

Here we enter a dangerous
and beautiful element
of the human experience…
you should know that
the people of your life are
not given or taken away
by accident…
The other human beings
that will become elements
in your spirit have been
placed in your path as
you have been placed
in theirs…

There will come enlightened
love spirits re-creating and
darkened hateful spirits in
decline. At this juncture we
are introduced to the dark
force of this world that
is a product of the most
primitive life cycles of
human evolution of
chance and change… This
penetrating evil spreads
unevenly over the
pulled and stretched veil
of the love spirit, and in
many souls becomes the
dominant life force.

This primitive evil force
must pull others into
its field to survive
and perpetuate itself…
As children we are not
born with this shadow
as many religions
would have you believe.
The creator love spirit
does not have any
elements of the shadow
in its light… but the
human experience has
created a shroud that

not only pulls and stretches
the love spirit but
replaces the broken
strands with its own
dark and ugly elements…
However, the love spirit
of life is very strong
and resilient, and
although the pressure
from the evil shroud
is relentless, it does not
overcome everyone…
In many it serves as
a means to vitalize and
draw the love spirit

by using the weight of greed
and evil against itself, and
serves to reinforce the
stronger spirit of human
communion with the
creator power of light and love…
So you will soon find
yourself in a field of
many types of souls:
the children's spirit still
alive and flourishing in
many adults, and the
hateful evil shroud that
has stretched and
weakened the souls of

other adults that must
pull from your energy
to keep their negative
shadow intact…
Because they are dispersed
throughout the very
breath of humanity, you
must be ever aware and
cautious to recognize them
in your life… They often
cloak themselves in beautiful
colors and words and
present the shroud in
deceiving and alluring
ways… Your love spirit

energy can be distracted,
and you will begin to
feel in your heart the
stretching of the fabric
of the veil and the
entry of the darkness…
At these times, you must
always seek out the
inner love that is your
very being and guard it
with your life's
breath… because you
see, at these moments
in your life's awakening,
it will be decided

if you must endure a
long painful life filled
with the shadow of despair,
or if you will be among
those that remain
in the love spirit of
light and take it
outside yourself to the
greater good of humankind
and join the ultimate love
spirit that humanity
has long been destined
to achieve… The adults
of light are among
you and your child

heart will be drawn to
them… The dark
hearts are also among
you and as a child
you may be forced into
emotional and physical
contact without a chance
to retreat… Again you
must remember that the
human beings that are
living in the shroud
are there because they
were pulled by the
negative human experience

so far that the shadow
became their being… you
must always try to
recognize and understand
this force of life… the
people driven by it
are, and will remain,
in the agony of darkness
until the light spirit
sees a moment of strength
that allows the beginning
of re-creation of the light
energy and the expulsion
of the fabric of hate…
Each of you can only
give this expression of

love and tolerance in
small ways but with
the children that remain
in the light and the
adults that grow
to the light, the future
of humankind will
realize a light again that
destroys the darkness forever.
So you see, these people in
your life that are of the
love spirit will be present
to teach and protect you…
and those in your life of
the dark shadow are there
for you to teach…

Earth

As you read these words,
more of life's elements
on our Earth are being
discovered in the deepest
reaches of the seas, in
caverns carved millions of
years ago, in ice caves eons
old and in the vibrant
rain forests, creatures that
have eluded humankind
for millennium… In the
most profound way our
very globe is the truest
example that nothing is
what it appears to be…

If a child held an orange
in its small hand and with
a tiny fingernail
dug out a little round
section of the peel, that
little piece of peel would
represent the scale of our
small Earth relative to the
orange ball of our Sun…
Still the very Sun that warms
us from millions of miles
away can be hidden
from view by that
same child's extended hand.
We are the very products

of many suns that carried
light, warmed organisms, and
formed life throughout the
billions of years of created
time… Our creatures, the
plants, the ability of
our Earth to sustain life
has been awarded to
humankind… This respon-
sibility is a love spirit
of godly magnitude and
it is no accident that the
shroud of darkness wants
only to shadow and destroy

the veil of love.
Our very place of
birth and breath, is
under attack by those
people that have
allowed themselves to
be torn and shrouded
in the darkness of
selfishness and greed…
To the children of the
spirit now being conceived
and born will fall the
task of halting the
demise of the energy
field we sustain our
very lives upon…

It is the calling of each
living child of spirit,
and adults that have
held tight to the love
spirit of life, to salvage
the creatures and living
energy of our patron
Earth… There have
been, and will be those
that hope to sacrifice
this bounty for the
sake of profit and
power, often in an
unforgivable rush
that does not allow

for study or alternative.
Always shrouded in a
guise of work and growth,
it is funded and furthered
in a rush to privilege…
Hidden often in the
development of progress
are those that need
to hold power over others
and in their need must
destroy the spirit source
of life for their indulgence
and life in the shadow and
their greed and power
must propagate more of the
same in the quest to
sustain itself…

Polished and dressed in many
cloaks it will look
like something good
or even noble, but in
fact, can be exposed
as the ritual death
of the life spirit itself...
However again, there remain
human beings with the
spirit of light that
continue to watch and
slow the oncoming
shadow that hopes to
consume the energy of
this Earth... They will

be joined by the children
of light spirit and
this struggle for the
very body of our
nature's energy cannot
be lost... Once the
creation force awarded
dominion over the Earth
it became humankind's
solemn duty to reign
in the elements of
darkness that will hope
to destroy it... Small
and large life systems
and creatures must be

held respectfully as elements
of the life force itself,
and destruction for
the enhancement of
power and greed must
be challenged at every
turn… This battle is
ours to continue… We
of the light spirit
must bequeath to
you this struggle for
Earth and life itself…

Church and Country

Now we must enter the
most dangerous threats
to your life's work of
maintaining the love
spirit within yourself…
The institutions of church
and country must be
combined because, although
you will be taught they
are separate, we
continue to learn that
nothing is as it seems
to be… We must be
very clear… church
and country are both

embroiled in a quest
for dominion over your
spirit and complete control
of your destiny!! Know
only that you are not
born into a religion
to be controlled by it… Nor
are you born into a
country to be owned as
a citizen… In truth
you are born into families
and geography as
children of the love
spirit to change and
rescue these systems from
the stranglehold of the

the darkness... not to
become slaves to their
dogma and decisions...
Both of these systems
can literally take your
life away... Again
camouflaged as faith and
patriotism, both church
and country will wantonly
take the desperate and
vulnerable sons and
daughters, often of the
poorest element, and
persuade them to kill
and be killed in the
name of the collective good.

Herein is the greatest sin
of mankind... to destroy
the very forms that
house and give breath
to the spirits... You
must never allow this
rape of your body and
mind; we call on you
to fight against it at
every moment, awake and
asleep... Begin now
teaching your subconscious
soul, in every thought, to
rebel against this
betrayal of God's
creating spirit...

Do not allow the seeds of
hatred and mistrust, thrust
upon you by clergy or
community… Stop cold in
every thought that is
orchestrated by church
and country that calls
for your spirit to
degrade another life…
Call out loud to the
communion of love spirits
continuously to halt even
the slightest march to
war…

The teachings of Jesus
the Christ, Mohammed,
the Buddha, Rumi, and
many enlightened souls,
including your very
own love spirit... cry
out for communion
between human beings
with love, respect, and
aid from suffering and pain,
as the only doctrine of
a life of spiritual and
material peace...

The very churches and
countries that hold
themselves unaccountable
for the balance of
humanity are completely
shrouded in the shadow
and have created the
most sophisticated and
dangerous illusions of
them all… Humankind
is dangerously close to
being overwhelmed by
the shadow force of evil.

In this reading, we are
opening every door that
can block the love spirit
from confronting and
challenging the darkness
of the shroud… None,
however, is as powerful
as the church and country
binary… The energy
pull they create is a
spiritual black hole out
of which the light of
love itself cannot escape.

We human beings, born
in the image and likeness
of the creator find ourselves
at the event horizon of
spirituality… The children
of this love and light
spirit, the adolescence
of love spirit, the
adults of the love spirit
and the aged that have
come back to the
collective spirit of light
and love are now
beginning to

breathe the breath of
the creator... That
sweet breath of knowing
that constricts and
shrinks the fibers of the
dark shroud that
hopes to overcome us...
This event horizon we
find ourselves at is
our call to unite as
human beings... We must
look carefully at the
leaders of church and
country to challenge

and discard each
angry and deceitful
spirit as they arise…
There are helpless and
desperate souls throughout
our world that are only
able to call out through
their spirit of love,
the cry hangs desperately
in the air of humanity…

This cry can only be
brought to bear
by the children and
adults of the spirit
of light that have
voice, and will, to
divert the human
spirit from the
precipice of destruction…

If You Are A
Young Human Being
You Already Know This.

Light and Darkness

"Lest we become again like
little children, we will never
know the kingdom of Heaven!!"
Matthew

Insight is a very difficult element
of the human life condition...
because as children we are forced
to rely on whoever is there to
care for us, we find attachment
to these people natural and in
the very elemental human sense,
satisfactory... This experience of
love exists even if the persons
given to care for us are irresponsible,
cruel, mean spirited, and even
abusive... because we are so
very helpless we must accept
dark and hurtful treatment
as acceptingly as caring and
loving treatment... Therefore, as
children we are forced into

'loving' exchange with other
people that direct our communion
with others throughout our
lives... Although we are aware
of physical pain when it occurs
or is dealt upon us... the emotional
pain inflicted upon children is
often mistaken, by the child,
for caring love and nurturing, and
even after the age of reason is
achieved; Some are still obliged
to continue in the relationship for
years further until finally able
to break the familial bond...
By this time the emotional
and physical communion with
other humans has become ingrained
and a form of exchange that
leads into like-type situations

in our relationship lives… Then
because the definition of love and
caring is shrouded in anger, hate,
cruelty and negativism the ones
some may gravitate toward tend to see
human exchange with the very
same start… Many, however, are
blessed with a family of love and
light and continue, throughout life,
to remain connected to the God spirit
of hope and trust…
These blessed souls gravitate toward
like spirited people and create a
life energy that attracts the same…
So you see, if you find yourself at
12± years old and surrounded by
despondent, mean, and dark-spirited
people, you may be entering an adult
life burdened with hardship and pain
that is self-fulfilling in your life's
relationship and energies.

Or if at 12± you find yourself
embraced by loving, creative,
dignified people of the love
spirit, you have been given the
greatest blessing of a life of
compassion and love…
But as is normally the case, you
will find yourself embroiled
between both types of people…
each drawing on energies in the
struggle for the enlightenment or
defeat of humankind…

In every child of light there
remains the warm core of emotion
that, even if hardened by abuse

and pain, can still distinguish
the fact that "I am not feeling
right about this person, place, or
activity"... This is the moment
when the miracle of love is opening
up within you to offer the vision
of a life without fears...
Take this warning to your very core...
The individuals that have imposed
their fear, pain, bigotry, and
disillusionment upon you were at one
moment in their life given the same
vision of life's missions and chose
to ignore the path of compassion
and strength to follow the
distrusting energy of the dark
elements... Often these same
people are so emotionally reined
into a vision of mankind that

all people, especially the children,
must be bent into the same
emotional slaves as they,
that it becomes the sole releases
of their human energies... I
will tell you now that every
society is laced throughout with
these types of powerful people
that will sacrifice any and
all light-minded to achieve
the overall state of negative
mind that is human and
justified in their lives!
For you see that given their
initial upbringing in life, often
divided by negative, darkened
emotional persons they had little
hope to break that bond of
fear when the warmth of love

presented itself to them… They
did not understand and therefore
did not break away from the
dark elements of the human
soul… Then once having chosen
a life in the dark realm the
people, places, things, and
activities in their life began
to reinforce the very disconnected
emotions they felt; and forced
them into masking emotions
of greed, lust, hatred, distrust,
and a host of additional emotions
that again serve only to
propagate the negative energy
they absorb and emanate…
But there is always hope in

the light of the spirits of
compassion—even the most
mean-spirited human can encounter
an event or situation that strikes
them with such a force of love
that their negative spirit can
be broken and like a dark
candle begin magically to produce
warmth and light… these spiritual
enlightenments can only be orchestrated
by a divine source that seems
to act only intermittently and
often it seems at random…
Therefore, this is your warning
that the moment in your life
when you will be open to

choose the light and compassionate
spirit, to follow into the
human experience, may come
upon you at any time… you
will sense an opening in the
fabric of your mind that will
help you know, beginning
now, your life choices will
lead you toward or away
from human love and caring.
However, now must come the
danger signals that are
at every moment in place,
and being repositioned, to lead
you away from communion with
people of the light and

human spiritual communion that
brings harmony with the Creator
spirit itself...
There is no gentle way
to break the following
life decision information to
you... this is simply the
way it is: you cannot believe
your physical emotions and those
of your parents and guardians
including your religious and
political superiors... period...
The intermingling of negative
and positive spirits, throughout
the human experience,
have created a family of
truths, near truth, near
falsehood, and pure lies

that permeate the collective
voice of human beings from
every culture, religion, music,
myth, and art... and to
begin to claim that one view
is the only view acceptable
is pure deceit and folly...
In the government of men
or souls the body elect
(by people of government
or by religious appointment)
are offering only
their version of a truth
or a lie as they have
interpreted it individually
or collectively and the
core issue of love, warmth,
and human respect cannot

be given a distinction as
a religious doctrine or a
governmental philosophy…
You see, every human
collection of laws and theology
to date has allowed: killing
if it's deemed necessary,
torture if it is deemed necessary,
pollution if it is deemed necessary,
genocide if it is deemed necessary,
violence if it is deemed necessary,
bigotry if it is deemed necessary,
and a host of additional dark
and negative soul conditions
to flourish in the name of
culture, faith, doctrine,
constitution, law and civil
obedience… Therefore, the

dark shroud of the human
soul is potential in every
human effort and more
often in consort with others
of the like-minded and
youthful experiences… So
you must know that for
the love of compassion
to emerge from the soul
of mankind (as a driving
and complete force) you
the children of the light
being born today must
know how to illuminate
this human madness
before we extinguish
ourselves in the name of
God, Culture, and Country!!

Love

Again we find that nothing
is what it appears to be.
The very senses that give us
the ability to progress as
human beings are the deepest
forces against our being able
to achieve success. Sight,
taste, feel, smell, touch, and
hearing are the vehicles that
cloud our ability to communicate
with the silent warm spirit
within… The paradox has
always been that we must
experience life through the

physical senses so it seems
possible to acknowledge and
verify the beauty as well as
the ugly elements of the
human soul… And because
it is necessary to survive
in the shrouded life of
human endeavors the senses
become the shield protecting
the enlightened spirit and
all that penetrates them in
the daily exposures are imprinted
in the negative and only the
warm chemical soup of the soul
itself can move the exposure

into a vision of light and
love of life… However, this
very essence of human nature
is always fighting its way out
of the challenges that are presented
through the collage of emotions
that are framed and sent
through these same senses…
When the child absorbs
a fragrance, a touch, a color
or a taste, it is always given
directly to the soul of
light and develops an aura
that becomes that smell or touch
and is recorded in a place of
life that can be viewed for

exactly what it is… Until that
same child is taught by someone
in their life the do's and do-not's
of culture, religion, or country,
then the same child will begin
to re-create a vision of the
taste and touch that is now
altered to fit the teacher's vision…
the innocence is lost… the creative
vision is tainted in the form of
the teacher's, priest, parents', officials'
vision… the shroud is placed between
the child-like soul and the
reality of the world… often
unfortunately, never to be lifted!

So how, a person must ask,
do we return to the purity
and innocence that the child
soul has created through the
initial contact with the
outer world through their God
given human senses of
sight, hearing, taste, touch, and
smell? This answer I'm afraid
is the most complicated and
difficult of all of life's paradoxes…
It is called, "falling in love."
Because we are in the material
world and subject to its elements
as they manifest themselves
around us, and only able to
judge through those same human
senses, for that very reason, we
are destined to complete

our enlightenment with the
limitations around us, to know
enlightenment exists among us,
and connect with another spirit to
allow us to enter the realm of
the spiritual light; this window
into the light of the Creator is
opened through the passion and closure
of being in Love... At the moment
of the infant's first breath, this
life of physical intimacy and structure
begins to take personal form, the
substance of human life is already
fully intact in the helpless infant,
all the evolved instincts that will
ensure the will to survive,
reproduce and communicate with
the outer world of humans, animals,
and life itself is fully intact and

hyper-sensitive to the new human
form and prepared to input all the
sensual sensations that will
serve those instincts in the
perpetuation of life... While consciousness is not yet opened, the core
mental and physical stimulus is
present to allow the infant to
organize the material human self
(even when it is dependant
on the mother and family for
every fundamental element of life).
The gentle understanding sensitivity
of the mother's touch, smell,
and taste is the foundation
for all infants' understanding of
human existence... Male children
and men will seek that same
sensuality throughout life and
female children and women will
find that same maternal instinct

in the lives of children and
their friendship with other
women throughout their lives.
In turn, the strong, clumsily
tentative touch, smell, and feel
of the father will become an
alluring and somewhat frightening
sensation that females will seek
to duplicate throughout life and
males will seek to both emulate
and separate from throughout their
life... Therefore, the relationship
between female children and
mother / father is always curious,
longing, and attractive, while
the male child's relationship is
functional, sensual, and with the intuitive
drive for dominance...
This remains the basis for child /
parent (guardian) exchange through
childhood and often into adulthood.

What happens to the child when
awareness and consciousness begins
to open in the child's mind is
that feeling, uninitiated and without
conscious understanding... that
somehow it is necessary to find another
person to begin to complete this
emotional and spiritual union that
is present throughout the living
realm from the smallest spark
of energy to the vast universe of
attracting stars and galaxies ... it
is a fundamental part of life
itself that attraction is necessary
to complete the form and give it
movement and energy...
It is also necessary for the
negative influence to be present
to stimulate the attraction. This
again begins the difficult and
sometimes trying relationship dance
that humans must do to

begin to recognize the true
love attraction when it finally is
presented…
The attraction / repulsion rhythm
starts very early in life and begins
to form in a conscious way as soon
as the child starts to lose the
sweet smell of innocence and
the physical body makes that
subtle transition into the
respective adult form. The
children feel the change as it
is happening and transforming
their very aware bodies into
a form they do not understand.
And during that most difficult
period, the emotional and
physical attraction / repulsion
stimulus is the most confusing
of all changes; girls often bond and
separate in emotionally strenuous
dramas and boys bond and

separate in physically violent acts,
both establish a hierarchy and
control and leave many, girl and
boy alike, in a state of aggressive
solitude... All of this, however, is
only to set the stage for
sexual attraction that is now
becoming the primary focus of
girl and boy alike... And the
artful motions of passion and
separation is set to begin.
If a grain of sand were suddenly
given legs and allowed to roam
the beaches of the earth in search of
the one exact mate to pair, its
plight would be no more futile than
that of all human beings' same
lifelong quest. You see, although
we are driven to seek that whole-
ness through another person, we are
powerless in the actual completion
of the quest... That is to say that
men and women alike, through countless

love cycles of passion / repulsion
beginning in the early teens and
continuing, often throughout
life, are striving to attach to that one
soul that will complete again that
childlike sensation of knowing and
love. And like the mobile grain of sand,
the search is often long, arduous, and
emotionally painful… The secret
lies in the ultimate human paradox;
that to glimpse and touch the
spiritual goal you seek, you must
trust that same spiritual dimension
to come of its own to you…
This source of trust is the key
to the expanding human experience,
the same power that created your
soul will present to you its pairing
in the course of your spiritual
journey… You will then realize
that all the matching completed
by your physical longings were

part of the material elements that
humans are born into, but
charged to elevate above… Therefore,
it is in the very quest for higher
personal spiritual understanding,
driven by the forces that have
grown in that very personal story
of your emotional struggles, failures,
and successes, coupled with the
light within, that you have been
bound to sustain; will provide the
essential inner strength that
will guide them toward that
spiritual connection that will
be manifest in your soul-person
that completes you, and you
will in turn complete.

The search initiated with the mind
is both futile and dangerous
and also unfortunately the primary
means that humans use to select
and form unions… This
leaves the world populated by
self-sustaining couples that are
bound together in the material
sense alone and therefore often
subject to the dark powers
of money, greed, and attracted to
the hateful bigotry of those that
strive for the same… Thus we
find the human world fraught
with those that feel hatred of the
power-less, poor, and destitute, and

often entrusted with constitutional
and dogmatic powers… These
self-attracted soul unions create a
gravitational pull that attracts
like unions into the very shroud
of darkness we are charged to
change!
The children of the light are
therefore the last vestige of
hope for the human experiment…
By conscious resistance
to the pull of materialism and
open hearted vigilance for the
personal spiritual path that draws
you to the soul person that will
unite you with yourself and
your creator and you in turn
will do the same for him or her.

Then this God / Creator union
will form their own attraction
field that will draw like
unions into the human core
that will become stronger and
more enlightened as a species...
Then we, the unions of children
of the light, can resist in every
field; constitutional, dogmatic,
institutional, and every other
approach toward materialistic
measure of human destruction.
We will find again the soul
of humankind that is charged
with gently raising the poor,
the creatures and the spirits
of life, up from the bondage

and pain inflicted by the
souls of darkness and greed…
This love of each other, through
the igniting of the lights
within, will surpass the
darkness and the shroud of
mistrust and hatred that
is at the edge of engulfing
the human structure… You,
today's children of the
light through the "In Love"
connection that is offered
through your own spiritual
perseverance and awareness
will allow humanity to finally
touch the fabric of God's being.

The blood of peace, trust, love, and joy for living will overcome the venom of the darkest souls and attraction will allow the living light to again prevail in mankind... That has been our charge since the beginning... All mankind has been progressing toward this very moment you are being born into. It has taken eons for the light to gain balance with the darkness, now it is possible for the darkness to be overcome in the very slightest way that will set in motion the salvation of all mankind.

Future

The task is formidable. There is
much allied against you.
Powerful corporations, religions,
and governments have much to
gain from poverty and ignorance that
provides labor and warriors to their
cause. Conflict and wars
build and maintain industries as
well as countries. The struggles
for the environment cannot be
fought by speechless animals
and fields of wilderness that
hope only to fulfill their destiny…
And throughout this all, there
are countless religions that will
want to direct your spirit according to
their particular mind, and the cultures
and government within which they
flourish will protect those religions at
the very expense of the spiritual
enlightenment in which they claim to
aspire.

There is finally the fullest
measure of hope that you,
the new ones of the light, will
seek out and recognize those that have
been holding the darkness at bay…
Those that are overcome by this
negative shroud will possibly begin
to understand what has changed
in them and they too will
see the inner light begin
again to erupt… We have
come, finally, to the place in
evolution where the peace and
hope of the inner child will
be strong enough to reclaim
the paradise of life… We
have been waiting for your

arrival, we have been holding
the negative world at bay,
recognize us and join us,
billions of children are the only
face of love that can prevail…

So there you have it… all that
we have to present has been laid
open for your review… If you read
this alone with your heart, it
will speak to the light, and
connect with those of the spirit,
if you openly exchange the vision
or seek its truth beneath a burka,
the words of law are the same
and they will enter your
consciousness and be introduced

to the living light within. And like the very molecules of oxygen that once were within the body of Christ, Mohammed, and many previous enlightened souls, will be endowed with the spirit of understanding and breathed out from your body, to be processed by our loving nature, and breathed in again by another soul, hungry and fearful, and maybe even shrouded in the darkness… This is the spirit exchange that begins with that first breath of innocence from the child of love and the spirit of light that will allow us to

finally prevail over the darkness
of the human condition…
Help us… breathe in the
breath of pain and despair,
process it with your spirit
and breathe out the breath
of love… The faint stars
of the physical world are
sending us their light waves
and particles of themselves,
the final sacrifice to give us,
the human spirit, the very
essence of life… We are
charged only with converting
it into love…

If you are a child of light,
regardless of your age,
You already know this!!

Printed in the United States
142321LV00004B/89/P